1-3 John

FROM DARKNESS TO LIGHT

NAME: _____

1-3 John

FROM DARKNESS TO LIGHT

Five Day Format

Each lesson is broken down into five separate days. This is only a recommended way to divide your study. A woman may use this breakdown or another of her choosing.

Memory Verse

Each lesson will include a memory verse on page 2. The memory verse should be learned for the week the lesson is discussed in your group.

Digging Deeper

For further study in to 1-3 John, give the section titled "Digging Deeper" a try.

Contributing Authors

1-3 JOHN, FROM DARKNESS TO LIGHT

Emily Dempster is serving as the Curriculum Coordinator for Salem Heights Church Women's Ministries. She earned her Masters in Pastoral Counseling through Liberty Theological Seminary University. She has a passion for discipleship in the church and seeing women's' lives changed as a result of God's Word. When given the chance, Emily loves watching her kids do whatever they are doing , traveling and exercising with her husband and two teenagers.

Julie Bernard serves as the Women's Ministries Director at Salem Heights Church. She loves the team approach to ministry and encouraging and developing women's leaders. She enjoys drinking coffee with friends, snuggling with her grandchildren, and golfing with her husband.

Angi Greene is involved in biblical counseling and enjoys ministering with her husband to couples preparing for marriage. She treasures opportunities to disciple and mentor women as she encourages them to love God and His Word. She loves spending time with her husband, daughter and two sons. Reading, running and baking are a few of her hobbies.

Chara Donahue has been married to Joe for 13 years and is usually busy chasing her four energetic children around. Chara is also a freelance writer, certified biblical counselor, and speaker. She has written for Christianity Today, iBelieve, (in) courage, and The Huffington Post, holds an MSED from Corban University, and is passionate about seeing people set free through God's truths. She is the founder and editor of Anchored Voices which aims to share the hope of Christ with the hurting heart.

Joanne Mueller loves God's Word and enjoys encouraging others to study the Bible for themselves. She earned her Bachelor of Arts degree in English, and, on most days, it is difficult to find any surface space in her home because every inch is cluttered with the various books that she has started reading. Her days are filled with her husband and two children who love to hike and fish in the Oregon outdoors.

Connie Libby works as the Women's Ministries Executive Assistant at Salem Heights Church. She is passionate about encouraging women in their relationship with Christ and delights in meeting their needs through Women's Ministries. Connie enjoys reading, sewing, cooking as well as camping and hiking with her husband and two teenagers.

Table of Contents

1-3 JOHN, FROM DARKNESS TO LIGHT

Workbook Lessons

1, 2 & 3 JOHN
Experiencing Transformation
INTRODUCTION TO THE STUDY

When someone is looking at a prism, they attempt to capture beams of light and angle them so that hidden colors will be revealed. Red, orange, yellow, green, blue, indigo, and violet come from a beam of white light that is separated into distinctive sections of the visible light spectrum. Rainbows are absolutely dependent on the light source. There is no beauty without the light. This is something that the apostle John, the author of the Gospel of John and the letters of 1-3 John, understood. He was there when Jesus said, "I am the Light of the world; he who follows Me will not walk in the darkness, but will have the Light of life" (John 8:12).

In fact, this preoccupation with light is one of the ways we are certain that John authored both the Gospel of John and the letters we will be studying. This son of thunder, the disciple that Jesus loved, this elder — John, never identifies himself by name as he writes his letters of encouragement and exhortation to the first century Christians in Asia Minor. In second and third John he calls himself "The Elder." In first John he offers no identification, but scholars agree that the style, theology, and vocabulary reveal the identity of the one who holds the pen behind the words inspired by the Holy Spirit.

The beloved disciple, who walked along the roads with Jesus, now speaks to the young church about truth, light, and love. He writes to convict, comfort, and convert. By offering three tests of authentic saving faith, love, righteousness, truth, John warns of those who do not love, obey, or hold to the truth and doctrine of the true Jesus, for it is by these things we can know who is truly following Christ. John reminds his readers, and us, of the richness of fellowship, and warns of those who seek to divide it. He lifts the hearts of the weary by pointing at the greatness of Jesus, the one who is fully God and fully man, and emphasizes the present dignity and future destiny of those who belong to Christ.

1

As you meditate on the Scripture throughout the study, and as God's Word adds color to areas that once were without, it is our prayer that you will also see how God has called you to reflect His glory in this world. We who are called "children of God" (1 John 3:1), are given the opportunity to reflect God's light together as the body of Christ onto the dull surface of a fallen world. As you proceed, ask God how you have been created and shaped through your experiences, and how you can use your talents and gifts to add the hues of truth, hope and love into a world soaked in lies, despair, and hate.

His light dwells within us, and like a prism which separates the different colors in the light spectrum, we are used to shine forth particular pieces of His character. Philippians 2:15 tells us that we "appear as lights in the world." As those made righteous through His Son to be His child, we hear His image to those who wonder, could that really be? Is there really a God that loves us all?

As you read John's letters, it is our prayer that your eyes will see and your heart will know more truth, more light, more love. That God would speak life into the parched and empty spaces of your soul and that you would trust in the hope that will not disappoint. Relationships fail, change comes, and dreams die, but Jesus was, is, and always will be enough. He is the one who lifts us from darkness and leads us to love.

LESSON 1

From Darkness to Light

Our eyes met as we walked toward each other in the supermarket parking lot. Time had passed, but I remembered her immediately. She and her young husband accepted Jesus on Easter Sunday. I heard the testimony of newfound faith years ago, but there were other things that came to mind as well; the grief in her eyes after her husband died, the heavy loneliness that seemed to nest in her heart, and that I had missed seeing her at church. We once worshipped together; I counseled her in her hardest time, but now our meeting had a hint of awkwardness.

She explained that she had met someone through a friend. He didn't know Jesus but was fun to be around. He soothed her lonely feelings, and because of the many hours they spent together, she felt cherished. He was able to provide her with a life of luxury that pacified the ache within her. Her time had been preoccupied with traveling alongside him and seeing the world. Due to the busyness of their schedule and the "guilty" feelings she felt at church, she had stopped attending and began avoiding those who had encouraged her in her young faith. She had found a temporary balm for her soul and had relinquished her search for the cure.

Many of us have reached for temporary fixes. We don't mind the darkness when it offers a false rest, but eventually we wake up to find the ache remains. John had seen many choose between darkness and light, and in 1 John 1 he clearly compares the actions of those walking in truth and those walking in darkness.

3

Day One

OUR JOY

1. Recall a specific time where you thought something would be one way, but when you experienced it, found it was different (i.e. vacation spot, job, relationship)?

Let's get started. Read all of 1 John today to gain a perspective of the entire book. A copy has been provided in the back of the book. Feel free to mark that copy or use your own Bible. There are a few common themes woven throughout the study; look for those. Underline verses found in the back of the book. Make notes as you read.

2. What are your initial thoughts and observations of the book? What themes do you uncover?

3. John doesn't introduce himself as the author of this book, but he does clearly state the purpose for writing it. What is his purpose (1 John 1:4 and 5:13)?

4. What is John proclaiming that "our joy" may be complete in? What might that look like in a life following Jesus?

5. What are you hoping to gain from this study?

Day Two

THE WORD

Read 1 John 1:1-4

6. John refers to Jesus in verse 1. What title does he give Jesus?

Jesus is called the same title in the opening verse of John's Gospel. Jesus is the living Word and is the communication between God and people. Think about it, God sent His Son so that we would have a way to communicate with and hear from God.

7. Turn to the back of the book. Circle the sense words in this passage (smell, sight, touch). List the words here.

"IN THE BEGINNING WAS THE WORD, AND THE WORD WAS WITH GOD, AND THE WORD WAS GOD."

JOHN 1:1

5

8. Why do you think John is using these sensory words here? Why is this important in the beginning of this letter?

9. 1 John 1:2 says, "the life was made manifest, and we have seen it, and testify to it and proclaim to you the eternal life, which was with the Father and was made manifest to us." How does the definition of manifest in the sidebar help you to understand what John is saying in this verse?

10. John uses this section of the book to inform readers that he actually saw, touched, and heard Jesus. This is different than the false teachers of his day who had not seen or known Christ. What difference does that make in how you respond to the remainder of his letter?

KEY TERM:

MANIFEST - TO PUT ON DISPLAY OR SHOW

"I AM THE RESURRECTION AND THE LIFE. WHOEVER BELIEVES IN ME, THOUGH HE DIE, YET SHALL HE LIVE, AND EVERYONE WHO LIVES AND BELIEVES IN ME SHALL NEVER DIE."
- JESUS
(JOHN 11:26)

11. The meaning of fellowship (verse 3) comes from the Greek word "koinonia" meaning: common, joint ownership and partnership. With whom does John desire his readers to have this fellowship?

12. What does the Gospel of John 17:3 say about this type of fellowship with God?

13. What does fellowship with God look like in your life personally?

Day Three

WALKING IN THE LIGHT

Read 1 John 1:5-10

14. What is John contrasting and proclaiming to Christians in this message?

15. What pictures come to your mind when you think about light and darkness?

16. In the chart below, organize what John says about light and about darkness from this passage into two columns.

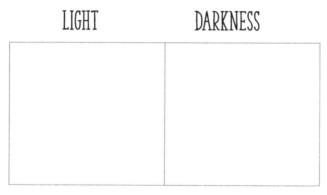

LIGHT	DARKNESS

What does this truth mean to you that God is light and there is no darkness.

17. What does John say about our fellowship with God when we are walking in darkness?

18. Is there an example from your own life where you might have tried to make living in the darkness work? What happened?

19. What about someone else? Do you see someone else who claims to have fellowship but is walking in the darkness? What two pieces of advice does Paul give us in Galatians 6:1? (Be careful to not share names in your group discussion.)

DIGGING DEEPER

Jesus speaks in the Gospel of John many times about light and darkness. Look at the following passages, what can you learn?

John 3:19 -

John 11:10 -

John 12:35 -

Day Four

FROM DARKNESS TO LIGHT

Read 1 John 1:5-10

20. John gives some "if statements" in this passage. Write them out here:

If we _____(verse 8)

If we _____(verse 9)

If we _____(verse 10)

21. Which of these is most difficult for you to understand? Why?

22. Why is it important to be honest with ourselves about our ongoing struggle with sin?

23. What kinds of sin do you personally justify and cover.

24. According to 1 John, what are the consequences of denying sin and walking in darkness?

What are the blessings and benefits of walking in the light and walking with God?

25. What is the difference between walking in darkness and the reminder from John that we all still sin?

26. Read verse 9. What is God faithful to do? What must we do?

Is there something you need to do right now?

We can walk in the light. There is no more hiding! Christ provided a way!

Day Five

LIVING IN THE LIGHT

Read 1 John 1:1-10

The great King David, whom God calls a man after God's own heart, spent a time walking in darkness. David had more than he could ever need. He had many wives and concubines as well as riches beyond measure. His heart longed for more, and when he saw from his rooftop the beautiful woman Bathsheba, wife of Uriah, bathing in her home, he couldn't resist but to send for her. He covered the incident by having her husband brought into battle on the front lines, and Uriah inevitably was killed. Nathan the prophet went to him and called him out, and in his confession, he wrote Psalm 51. Read this Psalm as David pours out his heart.

27. What can you learn about the character of God from this passage? How does that encourage you to walk in the light?

Before Christ, David would have needed to give up burnt offerings and sacrifices for his great sin to restore the fellowship he had with God. Today we have great victory in what Christ has done on the cross for us. Because Jesus came and died and rose again, we have direct communication with God. We are forgiven and can walk in the light.

28. Take time to reflect on what Christ has done for you. Write a prayer of confession like David did about those areas where you might be walking in the darkness. Ask the Lord to help you walk in the light.

LESSON 2

By This we Know

Not having an answer when it comes to health problems can be frightening, but the terror intensifies if a parent is watching a child suffer as the doctor pricks and prods. It is not only scary but heavy. Suddenly, the vast responsibility of caring for the sick floods in alongside a steadfast determination to find the answers that would lead to healing. The burden at times is overwhelming when doctor's answers are sought and a dead end is hit. It sometimes means turning around and looking for new roads that might lead to health. Second opinions are requested, medical interventions explored, and countless prayers are prayed by friends and family who join in the petition for healing. Tears are shed while heads are bowed, and through those pleas the Lord is sought. Exhausted, but without ceasing, a parent moves relentlessly with all their power to advocate for their sick child.

Day One

HE IS OUR ADVOCATE

Read 1 John 2:1-17

1. Think of the opening story and recall a time when you advocated for someone else either practically or in prayer. What did you do for the person, and how did he/she respond?

Read 1 John 2:1

2. John begins this chapter with an endearing term for his readers as he refers back to the statement he just made in Chapter 1. Read back over Chapter 1 and make a list of the truths about sin we learned last week. Based on those truths, why does John plead once again with his readers not to sin?

MEMORY VERSE

"BUT IF ANYONE DOES SIN, WE HAVE AN ADVOCATE WITH THE FATHER, JESUS CHRIST THE RIGHTEOUS. HE IS THE PROPITIATION FOR OUR SINS, AND NOT FOR OURS ONLY BUT ALSO FOR THE SINS OF THE WHOLE WORLD."

1 JOHN 2:1B-2

The good news about sin is: we have a Savior! John explains to our Father, Jesus is our advocate. This term *advocate* is unique to John's writings and is defined as: intercessor, controller and comforter. An example of a parent advocating for her child was used in the opening illustration.

3. When you think of Jesus Christ as your advocate, what thoughts come to mind? What times have you needed him as an advocate?

DIGGING DEEPER

Look up these other verses where John uses the term "parakletos" or advocate. It is also translated into English as "helper." What is unique to you about this term? How do you find hope and comfort that Jesus is our advocate?

John 14:16

John 14:26

John 15:26

John 16:17

4. In verse 1, Jesus is referred to as righteous. Why would this be important in relation to him also being our advocate?

5. In our sin, sometimes we feel guilty and turn away from the one who wants to be our advocate. We might feel like God is our enemy. Instead, John says Jesus is our Advocate when he is talking about sin. How does this resonate with you?

Where have you been hiding sin or justifying it for yourself?

Where do you need Jesus to intercede on your behalf? Use the sidebar and write a prayer of confession. Use 1 John 1:9 in your prayer.

JESUS LED A SINLESS LIFE AND TOOK THE WRATH OF GOD ON HIMSELF AS A SUBSTITUTE FOR ALL THE SIN OF THE WORLD.

"IF WE CONFESS OUR SINS, HE IS FAITHFUL AND JUST TO FORGIVE US OUR SINS AND TO CLEANSE US FROM ALL UNRIGHTEOUSNESS."

JOHN 1:9

Day Two

HE IS THE PROPITIATION

Read 1 John 2:2

KEY WORD:

**PROPITIATION -
A SACRIFICE WHICH
SATISFIES THE WRATH OF
GOD FOR OUR SIN.***

In this verse, we come across the word *propitiation*. Propitiation means, "a sacrifice which satisfies the wrath of God for sin." Not only is Jesus our advocate, John is telling his readers that Jesus satisfied God's wrath. The wrath that should be displayed to us for our sin has been satisfied on our behalf!

6. The other example of the phrase "is the propitiation" is used in one other place: 1 John 4:10. Look at this verse. Why is God willing to allow Jesus to satisfy His wrath?

7. When you think of this truth, that someone else would satisfy the wrath of God on your behalf, where do your thoughts take you? What would you want to do with these truths?

IN THIS IS LOVE NOT
THAT WE HAVE LOVED
GOD BUT THAT HE LOVED
US AND SENT HIS SON TO
BE THE PROPITIATION FOR
OUR SINS.
1 JOHN 4:10

How does knowing God's reason for propitiation add to your answer in question 6?

8. Not only did God sacrifice for you as an individual, according to verse 2, for whom else was Jesus the propitiation? How does this help you to view others?

Day Three

LIKE JESUS WALKED

Read 1 John 2:3-6

9. This section of John includes what is often referred to as the "Righteousness Test" of genuine belief. In other words, if you are walking in the light there will be evidence of righteousness displayed in your life. What are some of the evidences of the "Righteousness Test" according to John?

THE RIGHTEOUSNESS TEST: IF YOU ARE WALKING IN THE LIGHT, THERE WILL BE EVIDENCE OF RIGHTEOUSNESS DISPLAYED IN YOUR LIFE.

11. John contrasts these evidences with a strong statement in verse 4. What is the statement? Why do you think John says it so strongly in this passage?

12. John is not speaking of perfect obedience in this passage. If we were able to live perfectly, Christ would not have needed to die in our place. With that in mind, what is the difference between a growing believer who is living out these commandments and someone who just says they know Him?

13. Think about your own life. If you were to "walk in the same way in which he walked," how would you go about learning to do this? Where has God been showing you personally that you need to grow?

Day four

BOTH OLD AND NEW

Read 1 John 2:7-11

After addressing his readers affectionately once again, John brings up the old and the new to remind them of the command Christ has told all followers to obey. This is often referred to as the "Love Test" which Christ was the greatest example of.

14. Read Leviticus 19:18. What was the old commandant John was referring to?

THE LOVE TEST:
IF YOU ARE WALKING IN THE LIGHT YOU HAVE THE ABILITY TO LOVE OTHERS AS CHRIST WOULD.

Read John 13:34

This was not a new commandment, but "one that is fresh in quality, kind, or form; something that replaces something else that has been worn out. This commandment was 'new' because Jesus personified love in a fresh, new way, and it was manifested in 'believers' hearts and was energized by the Holy Spirit."[2]

15. Summarize what Jesus said in John 13:34.

16. What was fresh about Jesus sharing this old commandment?

17. What are some ways that Jesus loved others? What was different about that love?

18. John uses light and darkness again in this passage to contrast loving and hating a brother. What does it look like to love or hate a brother according to this passage (1 John 2:7-11)?

19. How are you doing at loving your brothers/ sisters in Christ?

Day Five

MARKERS OF MATURITY

Read 1 John 2:12-14

20. Record the groups John lists in this passage and the gospel truth in Christ in the chart below.

MATURITY LEVEL	CHARACTERISTICS OF MATURITY LEVEL

If you placed yourself in a category from the chart, where would you fit? Where would you desire to be?

Read 1 John 2:15-17

21. Returning to the moral implications of a transformed heart, what does John tell readers not to love (verse 15)?

22. Let's define the term "world" in the context of these passages. In verse 16, what does John say are the characteristics of the world?

1.

2.

3.

23. Use a Bible dictionary or an online resource to define each one of these and give an example of what that might look like in the life of a believer.

24. We can all struggle in each of these areas. Where do you struggle?

25. What does he say about the longevity of the things of this world?

26. In contrast then, what are we to love and what does he say about the longevity of a person that does the will of God?

Believers, we put much hope in the things of this world that are not everlasting. John encourages us to walk with God and to follow his ways because these have eternal value.

27. Thank God for eternal life and confess any areas you feel your heart straying over in the ways of the world.

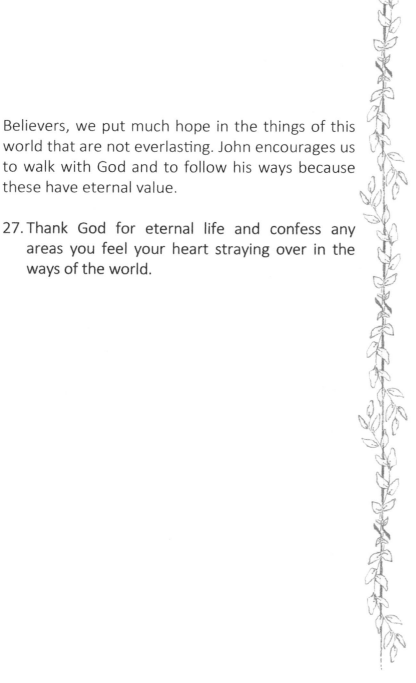

LESSON 3
Teach Me Truth

Every election season the term Antichrist gets tossed around by opposing sides, but it should not be used lightly. It is clear that this name projects the embodiment of evil to the church and ignites fear in the general population. What we often forget in considering the danger of the Antichrist's rise is that his demeanor will be one that seduces the masses. He will appeal to the longings of the world and offer himself as the solution, and he, like the devil, will be a master at deception and full of lies, but before he arrives there will be many who stand against Christ spreading messages that draw people away from God. John warns the church to be alert and wise when people come preaching philosophies that could distort and distract from the truth.

Day One

WAITING

Read 1 John 2:18

1. How would you live your life differently if you knew that this would be your last...

Hour:

Day:

Year:

John makes it clear that there is no time to waste. Time is a tricky thing, it moves on without our permission and refuses to stop at our demand. The New Testament authors viewed the coming of Christ and the completion of His work on the cross as the beginning of the end of this world. Here, 1900 years later, we are still waiting in this last hour, and there is no time to waste. In economics, time is considered a resource, but it is a relentless resource that takes no prisoners. It keeps ticking, as we wait for the day when all will be made right. So, in this last hour, we wait faithfully, full of hope for the coming day when the truth we stand for will be evident to all. While believers are actively taking part in the Kingdom of God and seeing it grow as more come to know the truth and love of Christ, we are also waiting for the Kingdom of God to unfold in its fullness. We often call this the tension of the "already" and the "not yet."

Read the scriptures and truth statements below, and write how each encourages you.

2. Christ will return, and He will not be late:

    Matthew 16:27

    2 Peter 3:8-10

3. No human will know when:

    Matthew 24:43-44

4. Be wise about how you use your time:

    James 4:13-14

    Ephesians 5:15-17

5. Look with expectant hope towards the future:

    Isaiah 25:8

    Revelation 21:4

Day Two

DEPARTING FROM THE TRUTH

6. Many people consider themselves anti-hate, anti-discrimination, and (hopefully) anti-murder. Thinking of how we use the prefix "anti" in daily life, what do you think it means?

Read 1 John 2:18-23

As we mentioned at the beginning of this lesson, a lot of fear surrounds the idea of the Antichrist (pronoun/singular), but notice the difference as John warns the church against antichrists (noun/plural). The antichrists John is warning this church of are those who are anti (against) Christ. They were prevalent in John's time and culture, and they are present in ours.

7. List three current common philosophies, or schools of thought, that are against Christ. (For example: The Bible is antiquated or old fashioned and must be read in light of a more progressive view).

    •

    •

    •

DIGGING DEEPER

Who is the Antichrist?
While John spoke of those who were against Christ as he discussed antichrists, there will be a capital "A" Antichrist. He will be an actual person who will reap much destruction on this world. Who is he? Look up the following verses to learn more.

Daniel 7:24-25, 2 Thessalonians 2:8-12 and Revelation 13:1-8

BY CONTRASTING THE ANTICHRISTS WITH THE BELIEVERS, JOHN ONCE AGAIN HIGHLIGHTS DARKNESS (ANTICHRISTS) AND LIGHT (CHRISTIANS - LITTLE CHRISTS).

8. In verse 19 John reveals his first indicator for identifying someone who is an antichrist. What is it?

9. While this verse gives warning, verse 20 offers hope for the perseverance of the saints and the eternal security of a believer. How so?

In what ways is this comforting? Or how might it stir up questions?

10. In verse 20, John also offers believers confidence in the power they receive from heaven by the anointing of the Holy Spirit. Write about a time when the Holy Spirit helped you discern between truth and falsehood (See John 14:26 to the side).

This letter is written to followers of Christ who are aided from falling into error by the Holy Spirit. In verse 21, John reassures them that he is confident in their ability to discern truth from lies. This is referred to often as the "Truth Test." In other words, if the truth abides in us we will show discernment in our beliefs.

11. Why do you think it was necessary that he wrote this warning about antichrists if he is sure of their knowledge of the truth?

KEY WORD:

ANOINTING - TO SET SOMEONE APART AND EQUIP FOR A TASK OF SPIRITUAL IMPORTANCE.

"BUT THE HELPER, THE HOLY SPIRIT, WHOM THE FATHER WILL SEND IN MY NAME, HE WILL TEACH YOU ALL THINGS AND BRING TO YOUR REMEMBRANCE ALL THAT I HAVE SAID TO YOU."
JOHN 14:26

TRUTH TEST:
IF YOU ARE WALKING IN THE LIGHT YOU WILL SHOW DISCERNMENT IN YOUR BELIEFS.

Day Three

ABIDING IN THE TRUTH

Read 1 John 2:22-25

12. In your opinion what is the most damaging thing about a lie?

Whoa John! Aren't you supposed to be the love guy? Why are you coming down so hard on these guys? Maybe they just need to be corrected and instructed. Isn't antichrist a bit harsh?

There are many people in today's society that would bristle with offense if you were to call them an antichrist but would have no issue with you saying they deny that Jesus was the Christ —both fully man and fully God. The term antichrist has long been associated with evil, and while Christians are those who have clearly recognized the potential for evil within them and their need to be saved, many others refuse to acknowledge the depravity within and need for redemption. They deny that the consequence of the bite of the forbidden fruit is evidenced in the brokenness of our world that we are faced with everyday. They hope their good will outweighs their bad and want to leave it at that.

Unfortunately, by denying the need of the gospel, they remain without redemption and are destined for hell. This is why truth cannot be separated from love — for by offering truth, we are extending the invitation into the greatest love ever known. The truth of the love that saves is Jesus the Christ.

13. John is working in a world of absolute truths, a concept the world has never been thrilled about. As we saw earlier in this study, we are not of the world. Here, in verse 22 John reveals his second indicator for identifying someone who is an antichrist. What is it?

14. **There is vibrant Trinitarian language happening in this passage.** In verse 22-25, we see John weave the relationship of Father and Son with the relationship that those who were given to the Son (believers) must abide in Him. Our memory verse is verse 24. Write out the meaning of this verse as you would explain it to a non-Christian friend.

TRINITY –
ONE GOD IN THREE
PERSON: FATHER, SON,
AND HOLY SPIRIT.

SO WHEN GOD DESIRED TO SHOW MORE CONVINCINGLY TO THE HEIRS OF THE PROMISE THE UNCHANGEABLE CHARACTER OF HIS PURPOSE, HE GUARANTEED IT WITH AN OATH, SO THAT BY TWO UNCHANGEABLE THINGS, IN WHICH IT IS IMPOSSIBLE FOR GOD TO LIE, WE WHO HAVE FLED FOR REFUGE MIGHT HAVE STRONG ENCOURAGEMENT TO HOLD FAST TO THE HOPE SET BEFORE US.

HEBREWS 6:17-18

15. What promise has God given those who abide in what they have heard from the beginning (the good news of the gospel)?

16. In order to live the abundant life, our moment by moment should be lived out in the freedom of abiding in these truths. How can you remind yourself of the truth of the gospel daily?

Take great joy in the fact that the promise of eternal life has been given to those who have the Father through acknowledging Jesus the Christ as Lord. And be at rest, for though lies swarm around us, in God there is no falsehood. He is trustworthy.

Day Four

DECEPTIVE TEACHING

Read 1 John 2:26-27

17. In this section of scripture, John reveals his third indicator for identifying someone who is an antichrist. What is it?

18. List all three indicators seen this week:
    1.

    2.

    3.

19. Is John saying that we do not need other people to instruct us in verse 27? Scripture does not contradict itself, and Ephesians 4:11-12 and Colossians 3:16 both address the importance of the body of Christ teaching one another. John is teaching them in his writings, but he is also warning them about outside instruction taking them away from the truth of the Gospel. Why is the Holy Spirit the most reliable teacher of truth?

20. How can false teachers damage the church? How can they be dangerous to unbelievers?

Have you seen this in your own life or the lives of the people around you? What impact did it make?

Take a moment to pray for someone you know who has been hurt by the false teachings of someone against Christ.

21. Read the following passages of Scripture:

John 16:13 and 1 Corinthians 2:11-16

What is the anointing received from God that abides in the follower of Christ?

22. What does this anointing aid you in doing? How does this encourage you as you pursue truth?

NOT ONLY MUST WE ABIDE IN GOD, BUT HE ABIDES IN US.

Having the Holy Spirit gives us confidence as we encounter false teachers! What a privilege to have as we go forward in a world full of anti-christs.

Day Five

ABIDING IN CHRIST

Read 1 John 2:27-29

John, a fisherman and "son of thunder," spent much of his recorded life encouraging believers to stay close to, abide in, and love Jesus. In the Gospel of John 15:4-5, he reminds readers that Jesus tells us, "Abide in Me, and I in you. As the branch cannot bear fruit of itself unless it abides in the vine, so neither can you unless you abide in Me. I am the vine, you are the branches; he who abides in Me and I in him, he bears much fruit, for apart from Me you can do nothing."

We must remain connected to our soul's life source, our Lord, our God. As we abide in Christ and the Spirit abides in us (as seen in verse 27), we are fueled with supernatural strength to do the work of God. Not only does our ability to discern between truth and lie increase, but also our heart begins to find a home and take rest in the love of our Savior.

23. What reassurance (verse 28) does John say we will receive as we abide in Christ?

24. Why will some people be ashamed before God when he returns to this world of victory? How does the world say we should live? Reflect in what areas you are abiding or living for self.

25. In verse 29, John discusses the righteousness of God as fact, but often instead of accepting God for who He says He is, people begin to let their idea of God be shaped by who they think He should be. They begin to craft a God of their own making - *in their own image.* We see this when people excuse their sin by assuming that God will release His requirement for holiness. Underneath are listed some common lies. Why is each of these faulty according to scripture?

- "God will understand how bad I wanted this."

- "Holiness (or God's wrath) is just an old fashioned idea."

- "God just wants me to be happy."

26. When Christ appears, do we really want to have a form of the serpents question, "has God said" (Genesis 3:1) falling from our lips? Often we believe lies that keep us from God's righteousness without realizing it. Take time to ask God to reveal any lies you believe and thank Him for the Spirit that abides in you.

27. Were you able to identify a place in your life that you know you are questioning God? If so, what was it? Can you find a place in scripture that gives you truth to conquer the lie?

LESSON 4

Tests of a True Believer

Our love often runs deep for our favorite things, but they can be quickly swept away when that thing no longer serves us the way we desired it to.

Oh, how great my love is for ice cream...until my pants no longer fit. How great my love is for my new phone/TV/car...until the next version comes out. How great my love is for my church, until they make me confront my sin.

We are human; our love is imperfect. We long to offer unconditional love, and while we may extend moments of the patient, sacrificial, flawless love that God bestows on us, we will do it imperfectly this side of heaven.

How faulty and temporal my love...
How fickle my affections...

The prosperities for the human heart to stray from the ways of God do not surprise John, and throughout his letter he continues to exhort the church through truth and love to stay focused on Jesus as they learn to guard against those who teach a different gospel. He reminds readers of the three tests that will help the church evaluate their own hearts as well as the validity of those who enter it: The Righteousness Test, the Love Test, and the Truth Test.

Day One

UNKNOWN TO THE WORLD

1. Think of a moment you felt truly loved by another person. What qualities do you believe made that moment stand out among others? Do those qualities reflect any of God's characteristics?

Read 1 John 3:1-23

2. John tells us that because we are children of God, the world will not know us. What do you think this means? Write your answer as if you were explaining verse 1 to someone else. *When John says that "the world does not know us, " he means that...*

DIGGING DEEPER

Both John and Paul (author of multiple other New Testament books) highlight the importance of believers knowing they are children of God, but they approach it from different perspectives. Paul often comes from the legal standpoint of here are the things that are true about you and your inheritance because God had adopted you into his family, whereas John uses terms like "born of" (1 John 2:29) and "because His seed abides..." (1 John 3:9).

Look up Romans 8:14-17, Ephesians 1:3-9, and Galatians 4:1-7 and contrast how Paul and John have talked about being children of God. What do both view points tell you about your standing on God's family?

3. John gives us some beautiful identity statements in verse 2.

   Who does John say we are?

   Who does John say we will be (like)?

Such hope resides in the fact that there will be a day where we will be fully conformed to the image of our perfect Savior. Though words fail to describe what the days that live beyond our imagination will look like, it is safe to say that we will be left in awe of the glory we have yet to behold.

4. Often our eyes are focused on temporal things, but in verse 3 we are reminded that hope for being completely pure will someday be realized. In the meantime may we desire to continually be like Jesus and daily be made more like Him. Take a moment to pray this prayer of David from Psalm 51:10-12 for yourself:

"Create in me a clean heart, O God,
And renew a steadfast spirit within me.
Do not cast me away from Your presence
And do not take Your Holy Spirit from me.
Restore to me the joy of Your salvation
And sustain me with a willing spirit."

Day Two

PRACTICE RIGHTEOUSNESS

John loves to flirt with the abstracts and mystery that is woven through our existence, but as he speaks of lofty things that are often hard to define: righteousness, love, truth, he breaks it down as an elder to his children. *Here is how you must live. Here is what you must do.* While allowing ourselves to be swept into the marvelous things of God, we must also be willing

to see that sometimes the ways God brings the abstract into the practical is through simple, faithful acts of obedience.

> Read 1 John 3:4-10

5. In verse 4, we are reminded that in Jesus there is no sin. What a relief, since yesterday we looked at how we will be like Him...someday. That *final day* is not *today,* however, so how do we take a statement like "no one who sins has seen Him or knows Him" in verse 6 and reconcile that with our own fallen/redeemed humanity?

6. What word do you see in verses 4, 7, 8 and 10 that gives you a clue of what John is looking at when he looks for righteousness in a believer?

7. We often hear the adage, "practice makes perfect," in our culture as we try to learn new skills. What does practicing sin look like? How do you practice righteousness?

8. The Bible promises us that we are made into new creations when Christ becomes Lord in our lives (2 Corinthians 5:17), but this does not mean we never sin again. Refer back to 1 John 1:9-10. How should we as believers deal with sin when it happens? (Notice the question says *when*, not *if*.)

9. In verse 10, John says, "anyone who does not practice _____ is not of God." This Righteousness Test is the first of three tests we will look at in this week's study. Think of someone you know to be a practitioner of righteousness. What about this person's life made you think of them?

THE RIGHTEOUSNESS TEST: IF YOU ARE WALKING IN THE LIGHT, THERE WILL BE EVIDENCE OF RIGHTEOUSNESS DISPLAYED IN YOUR LIFE.

Day Three

THE EXAMPLE OF CAIN AND ABEL

Read 1 John 3:11-12

Like John's reminder in these verses, we must constantly admonish and encourage the church to love one another. Jesus told us that, "By this all men will know that you are my disciples, if you have love for one another." (John 13:35)

WHEN MY FACE HAS FALLEN, I WILL LIFT MY EYES TO THE GOD WHO SEES, LOVES, AND COMFORTS. THOUGH MY SPIRIT MAY BE WEAK, HE IS ALWAYS STRONG.

Love is evangelistic. It takes what the world does not know (verse 1) and makes it evident. However, when people who are operating out of the flesh instead of the Spirit have their deeds, which were kept in darkness, shone upon by the light, they do not always respond well.

Read the story of Cain and Abel in Genesis 4:1-16. Note that: *"...Cain became very angry and his countenance fell"* (verse 5).

10. Why was Cain angry?

11. Why do people sometimes act or feel like the righteousness of a brother or sister is a threat to them?

How is this in opposition to the ways of God?

"Then the Lord said to Cain, 'Why are you angry? And why has your countenance fallen? If you do well, will not your countenance be lifted up? And if you do not do well, sin is crouching at the door; and its desire is for you, but you must master it'" (verse 6 and 7).

12. What can we learn from God's words to Cain when we face consequences for our actions that stir our anger and cause our face to fall?

13. Did Cain master sin or let it rule him?

14. What did Cain's choice cost him?

15. According to 1 John 3:12 why did Cain choose to slay Abel?

Imagine what Cain's life would have looked like if he had chosen to obey God and love his brother while still dealing with the emotions at war within himself. Though we could never know the implications of what that would have meant for humanity, it is clear that Cain chose his own way over God's and evil quickly progressed.

16. What have you learned from visiting the story of Cain and Abel?

Day Four

LOVE

Read 1 John 3:13-18

Just as the righteousness of Abel made Cain threatened, sometimes the righteousness of believers shines light onto the darkness of unbelievers, which can lead them to jealousy or hate. Our very actions may lead people to call us judgmental, not because we have judged, but because they then judge themselves and don't want to look at their own depravity. This is just one reason the world will hate those who seek to follow Christ. Another reason the world might hate Christians is that they find us hypocritical. They do not understand that we freely admit we are sinners saved by grace and depend on Jesus to be our righteousness. We are in the process of becoming more like Him.

17. What other reasons might the world give for hating those who follow Jesus?

18. Here we see another "Love Test." How does John say we will know that we have passed from death to life in verse 14?

THE LOVE TEST:
IF YOU ARE WALKING IN THE LIGHT, YOU WILL HAVE THE ABILITY TO LOVE AS CHRIST WOULD.

Why is the ability to love others supernatural?

19. John says, "Everyone who hates his brother is a murderer, and you know that no murderer has eternal life abiding in him" (verse 15). Read Matthew 5:22-28. Should we be more concerned with attitudes or behavior? Why?

WHEN HATE PRESSES IN, WE ARE SHIELDED BY OUR MIGHTY GOD AND CAN REST IN THE LIGHT OF HIS LOVE.

20. John 3:16 tells us how deeply loved we are, "For God so loved the world, that He gave His only begotten Son, that whoever believes in Him shall not perish, but have eternal life." 1 John 3:16 tells us what love is and looks like. How was this love first demonstrated? How can we show it (verse 16 and 17)?

21. In verse 14, John says, "He who does not _____ abides in death." This is the second of three tests of a believer that we have looked at in this week's study. Think of someone you know to be a practitioner of love. What about this person's life made you think of them?

Day Five

TRUTH

Read 1 John 3:18-23

22. In what ways are we to love and not to love (verse 18)?

What would loving only by words look like? What is an example of deed and truth?

23. How can we be confident that we love correctly (verses 21 and 22)?

24. How do verses 21 and 22 assure your heart?

25. In verse 18, John says, "Little children, let us not love with word or with tongue, but in deed and _____" The Truth Test is the final test of a believer in this week's study. Think of someone you know to be a practitioner of truth. What is evident in this person's life that made you think of them?

THE TRUTH TEST:
IF YOU ARE WALKING IN THE LIGHT, YOU WILL SHOW DISCERNMENT IN YOUR BELIEFS.

26. Recall all three tests mentioned in this lesson.

1.

2.

3.

27. Which one might you be mindful of practicing this week?

LESSON 5
Living Loved

Little Naomi. Just barely four years old with sunken sad eyes, she laid her head on my lap. I felt the fever, but I knew that hollow look came from much more than the virus her little body was fighting off. She had just recently arrived at the orphanage, having been rescued from those who hurt her and were training her for prostitution. She did not know love, and it was written across her face. My heart broke when I had to leave her. Oh, how I wanted to scoop her up and bring her home. A year later when I returned, my eyes searched frantically for Naomi; I found her! That little frail girl was now bouncing around with joy and mischief written in her eyes and across her face. What had changed? She had experienced love for the first time, and it had changed EVERYTHING!

God had rescued her and put her in a place where others loved her and provided a safe place for her. Fear no longer lingered in her eyes. She was now living loved.

Just as Naomi was changed by human love, our lives are radically different when we know God's love. God wants us to live as though we are loved, because we are! We are no longer orphans; no longer do we have to live in fear. Our Father loves us perfectly and completely. John repeats this message over and over so we won't miss it. God's love settles us down and is the impetus for our love for others.

Day One

TRUTH OR A LIE?

John must have been concerned for his readers. He expands on his warning of false teachers in 1 John 2:18-28 and in 1 John 4:1-6. Gnostic teaching was infiltrating, and John desired to provide specific, fail proof tests to help believers discern false teaching and turn from it. This is considered another Truth Test.

1. When have you been told something and later found out it wasn't true?

Review 1 John 2:18-28 and Read 1 John 4:1-6

2. Why is it imperative for believers to be on the lookout for false teachers?

3. What tests does John encourage believers to apply to every teaching to determine if it is true?

GNOSTICS BELIEVED IN ACQUIRING SPECIAL, MYSTICAL KNOWLEDGE AS A MEANS FOR SALVATION AND PURSUING GOODNESS INSTEAD OF SEEKING A NEW LIFE IN CHRIST.

"BELOVED, DO NOT BELIEVE EVERY SPIRIT, BUT TEST THE SPIRITS TO SEE WHETHER THEY ARE FROM GOD..."

1 JOHN 4:1A

4. Do you regularly evaluate what you hear to determine if it's true? How does Hebrews 4:12-13 encourage you to be discerning?

5. Despite the abundance of false teaching what reassurance does John give? In what ways does this encourage you?

Day Two

PROVEN LOVE

Read 1 John 4:7-10

John moves past deciphering false teaching to the action of love, along with the proof and evidence of true love. This love is from God, is God and has been proven by God. This love makes ALL the difference in a believer's life.

6. The love John mentions is referred to in Greek as "agape" love. This love is not based on feeling or even friendship. It is a selfless, sacrificial and unconditional love. What action did God take because of His love for mankind?

7. Read more about this love in John 15:13 and Romans 5:6-8. How did Jesus prove his love? What difference does it make to you today to know that God has already proven His love for you?

8. What benefits of God's love does Paul mention in Romans 5:9-11?

9. Love is a part of God's character. John says, "God is love." Take a moment to praise God that He is love and thank Him for the evidence in your life of His love for you.

Day Three
LIVE LIKE YOU'RE LOVED

God's perfect sacrificial love impacts our lives so significantly that we will live differently.

Read 1 John 4:11-12

10. What will be true in our lives as we recognize and accept God's love for us?

11. Why are we called to love one another?

12. Read 1 Corinthians 13:4-8a and Colossians 3:12-14. What is our love for one another to look like?

13. Consider those in your life that are difficult to love. At the same time consider God's love for you. In what ways does God's love for you encourage you to love them?

14. John says God's love "is perfected" in us. "Is perfected" means to bring to completion, to accomplish, or finish. What will be the evidence of God's love accomplishing its purpose in your life?

GOD COMMANDS US TO LOVE BECAUSE HIS SPIRIT LIVES IN US AND LOVE IS A PART OF HIS CHARACTER AND A FRUIT OF HIS SPIRIT.

Day Four
HE IN ME

Left to love others out of our own initiative and care leads to love that is manipulative and self-serving. God does not ask us to love others because they deserve it or out of our own generosity and selflessness. God commands us to love because His Spirit lives in us and love is a part of His character and a fruit of His Spirit.

Read 1 John 4:13-16

15. What does John say we can know?

16. How can we be confident in these truths?

KEY TERM:

ABIDE - PORTRAYS THE IDEA OF SETTLING DOWN, BEING AT HOME, AND CONTINUING IN RELATIONSHIP.

17. John and the apostles saw Christ's death and resurrection with their own eyes (verse 14). Although we did not witness this event, we believe by faith it happened. What takes place when we believe (verse 15)?

18. How does John describe the relationship between a believer and the Holy Spirit? For further insight consider John 15:4-5.

19. What can we know and believe as a result of God's Spirit abiding in us (verse 16)? How does this knowledge impact your relationship with God? With others? Your view of yourself and your circumstances?

DIGGING DEEPER

Look up the "one another" statements in the Bible. What do you discover about how love acts when we live alongside and interact with one another.

Day Five

LIVING FEARLESS BECAUSE OF LOVE

Only God's perfect love can cast out fear (1 John 4:18). To live loved, is to live secure, safe in God's love, and free to love others. John wraps up this section on love with encouragement and a charge to action.

Read 1 John 4:17-21

TO LIVE LOVED IS TO LIVE SECURE, SAFE IN GOD'S LOVE, AND FREE TO LOVE OTHERS.

20. What results can we expect when we understand God's perfect love for us (verse 17 and 18)?

21. If we are living in fear that our eternity is not secure or that our sin is too much for God to forgive, John tells us we do not understand God's love for us. Read the parable of the prodigal son in Luke 15:11-24. Make note of the father's attitude and action toward his run -away son.

22. How does the example of the father help you to understand God's love for you?

23. How would an accurate understanding of God's love put away any fear or doubt you may have about God?

24. When we abide and are at home in God's love for us, we are free to love others. Review verses 1 John 4:7-21. List reasons believers are to love others.

25. Consider your own motivation for loving others. Does it line up with the reasons John gives in these verses? Why or why not?

26. Meditate on God's love for you. Thank Him and ask Him to help you to love others simply because He first loved you.

LESSON 6
A Firm Foundation

The foundation is the most important, though not the most exciting, component of a home. It gives the building stability and shapes the structure. If there is fault in the foundation, walls might crack, windows could break, and porches separate from the home. A weak foundation leads to damage and disrepair, but a well-crafted one can support a building for hundreds of years. The home itself testifies to the understructure that offers the support needed to survive heat, storms and earthquakes. As the elements press in, the walls remain straight, the floors don't sag and the structure remains sound.

Our spiritual lives must be given a foundation of faith in Jesus Christ and the power of the transforming work of the Gospel if we hope to stand when the fallen world rains down. When a life is built on the firm foundation of the truth of Christ, there will be noticeable evidence in the life of a believer. Also, the object of real faith is Jesus Christ.

Day One

REAL FAITH COMES FROM KNOWING THE TRUTH

1. If you could hunt for any treasure, what would it be? What important facts would you need to know in order to be successful?

John wraps up this letter with a summary of the common themes he presented throughout the book.

Read 1 John 5:1-12

2. What topics/themes mentioned in this passage has John already addressed in 1 John?

3. Why do you think John has been repetitive?

4. Which themes have been most encouraging to you? Why?

5. How has your thinking about the Christian life changed as a result of this study so far?

Day Two

RESULTS OF REAL FAITH, LOVE AND OBEDIENCE

Throughout 1 John, discernable characteristics of saving faith have been presented clearly. What we believe will influence how we behave. In this section of Scripture, John again highlights love and obedience as markers of real faith.

Read 1 John 5:1-3

6. When someone believes that Jesus is the Christ, a fundamental change happens. Look up the following verses and record the truths about those that trust Christ for salvation.

Ephesians 2:1-6

Colossians 1:13-14

2 Peter 1:2-4

7. How do these truths enable us to obey His commandments?

8. Upon salvation, we are born into the family of God. List the characteristics of one "born of God" found in verses 1-3. Add any references from previous lessons.

9. How does loving God translate into love for fellow believers?

10. What does that look like in your life?

11. How does keeping God's commandments reveal love for the Lord?

12. What habits in your life help you to grow in your love for the Lord?

13. What does John mean when he says in verse 3, "his commandments are not burdensome?" What commands is he referring to?

14. Why should obedience to God not be a burden to believers?

Day Three

ANOTHER RESULT OF REAL FAITH-VICTORY

Read 1 John 5:1-4

In this section, John again uses the phrase born of God; the idea that at salvation we are born into God's family and now share His nature. Salvation changes us. We have a new nature and the new potential to live in a way that honors Him. John introduces the truth that believers are overcomers. Victory over sin is another discernable mark of real faith.

15. In verse 4, what is another description of "one who overcomes"?

16. Read John 16:33. What truth did Jesus tell his disciples should bring them peace and encouragement while living in a hostile world?

17. Why does faith in Christ assure believers victory over the world?

DIGGING DEEPER

Find other places where the word "overcome" is used in 1 John. What did you learn from your study?

18. Which of the following statements are true of you most of the time?

    A. I hope I can obey God today. I'm going to try really hard, but sometimes the temptations are just too much.

    B. I am thankful that I can obey God today because I belong to Him and He will help me live out the victory over sin that He has already secured.

19. How would starting from a position of victory give you confidence in God's ability to help you walk in obedience?

Don't miss the great power in this passage: Believers have victory over the world! Because those who believe in Jesus Christ are born of God, they share in the victory Christ had over sin and death when he accomplished the work on the cross. Faith in Jesus Christ assures believers that they are empowered by the Holy Spirit to have the ability to walk in obedience. This does not imply we live perfect, sinless lives while here on earth. The battle between the old nature (the flesh) and the new nature remains. But the overall direction of a believer's life will be one of victorious living by God's power. Where there is sin present, confession and repentance follow and fellowship and joy in the relationship is restored.

Day Four

REAL FAITH-IT'S FOUNDATION

If believing that Jesus is the Christ is what brings about salvation, it is important to know with certainty that the object of faith is true and real. In this section of Scripture, John presents evidence that both historical fact and evidence of a changed life as a result of the Holy Spirit living in a person can provide that certainty.

The doubters of the day were called Gnostics. They did not believe that Jesus was God; they instead believed that He was given divine nature while on earth. If this were true, Jesus lacked the authority and ability to accomplish salvation because the death of a mere man would not prove anything.

Read 1 John 5:6-12

20. John identifies three "witnesses" through which God the Father provided evidence for the historical fact that Jesus is the Christ. Complete the chart on the next page.

REFERENCE(S)	WITNESS	EVIDENCE THAT JESUS IS THE CHRIST
Matthew 3:13-17	*The water-* refers to Christ's baptism	
Matthew 27:51-54 Mark 15:33-39 John 12:27-29	*The blood-* refers to Christ's death	
John 14:26 John 15:26 Ephesians 1:13-14	*The Spirit-* Refers to the Holy Spirit	

21. 1 John 5:8 says these three witnesses are in agreement. How does the evidence from the chart support that Jesus is the Son of God?

While God's testimony concerning Christ is the most important, a believer's life story will also point to the fact that faith in Jesus brings salvation and transformation.

22. In what ways does your personal testimony give evidence of the transforming power of faith in Jesus Christ?

Day Five

REAL FAITH TRANSFORMS

What we believe is important; it is called doctrine. How we live is also crucial. Our lifestyle can either support our beliefs or work against them. Real faith will produce evidence of transformation. What we say we believe is demonstrated through our attitudes and actions. Our belief and lifestyle will complement each other.

Review 1 John 5:1-12

23. Look at these examples and fill out the chart below:

VERSE	WHO	EVIDENCE OF A TRANSFORMED HEART
Luke 19:1-10		
Acts 9:1-22		

24. What is amazing about these stories?

REAL FAITH WILL PRODUCE EVIDENCE OF TRANSFORMATION.

25. Thank God for the transforming work of His Spirit in your life. Thank Him for this awesome evidence that the Spirit is needed and real.

LESSON 7

Some Things We Know For Sure

Certainty. Assurance. Confidence. What images come to mind when you read these words?

The reality is we live in a world that is full of unpredictability and uncertainty. We all have areas in life where certainty would be a welcome guest, but there are few things in life that we can "bank on." When it comes to faith, there is clearly mystery involved, but John wants believers to find rest in the assurance of salvation. Too much is at stake, and an ambiguous faith does not lead people into the great adventure that God intends. Risk. Trust. Freedom. Confidence of salvation helps a believer step into the unknown with assurance.

As we begin to study these last few verses of 1 John, we will find a call for believers to enjoy their salvation with certainty. Inspired by the Holy Spirit, John desires for believers to be in a place of settled confidence. God's desire for His children is that they trust not only in His ways, but also in His love.

Day One

YOU CAN KNOW FOR SURE:
YOUR SALVATION IS REAL

1. If you were guaranteed a proof positive answer, what one question would you want answered? Why?

Read 1 John 5:13-21

2. List the things John wants the readers to "know"?

3. Underline the word "know" in the passage at the back of this book. What does the repetition of the word tell you?

4. Why do you think certainty about these truths is important for a believer?

MEMORY VERSE:

"THESE THINGS I HAVE WRITTEN TO YOU WHO BELIEVE IN THE NAME OF THE SON OF GOD, SO THAT YOU MAY KNOW THAT YOU HAVE ETERNAL LIFE."

1 JOHN 5:13

KEY WORD:

TO KNOW–TO UNDERSTAND AND BELIEVE WITH CERTAINTY, ASSURANCE AND CONFIDENCE

In similar fashion to the Gospel of John, in 1 John readers are given a purpose statement which summarizes his goal in writing. In the Gospel of John, it was written, "so that you may believe that Jesus is the Christ, the Son of God, and that by believing you may have life in His name" (John 20:31). In John the truth that Jesus is God's son and that He is the only way to eternal life with God was laid out. John's purpose for writing 1 John was different. The Spirit of God instructed John to write 1 John so that the believer would know to the deepest parts of their existence their soul is saved, making their joy complete.

Read 1 John 5:13

5. The phrase "these things" is referring to all that has been written in 1 John so far. What are the major topics in 1 John that have been presented so far which present evidence of salvation?

6. Why is it important for you to be confident in your salvation?

7. When you are tempted to doubt your salvation, what is the outcome in your daily life?

79

Day Two

YOU CAN KNOW FOR SURE: GOD HEARS YOU AND WILL ANSWER!

Read 1 John 5:13-18

Prayer is a beautiful spiritual discipline, for it is the means by which we communicate with the God of the universe. Someday in Heaven, believers will communicate face-to-face with God. This side of heaven our minds can't contain the splendor of what this will be like, but still, in the here and now, we have been given prayer which gives us access to the abundant resources of Heaven. We send requests, and our God sees; He hears. As our minds are renewed by His work and our hearts are transformed by His Spirit, our prayers become more aligned with His will, and we can move forward with confidence that He is with us.

CONFIDENCE IN PRAYER COMES WHEN WE ASK ACCORDING TO GOD'S WILL.

8. When a believer prays according to God's will, what two things can be known with certainty?

9. Based on these verses, how would you answer someone who claims that God has not answered their prayer? How does 1 John 3:21-24 add to your answer?

Read 1 John 5:16-17

Have you ever seen someone committing sin? What did you do? When a brother or sister is caught in sin, we know we are to restore them gently (Galatians 6:1). Here we are also reminded that we must pray. John is calling us to the great joy and power that is in intercessory prayer. By praying for others, we get to take part in God's redemptive plan. He is also identifying one scenario in which prayer will not be time well spent.

It is clear that the readers of John's letter know exactly what he is talking about, but for those of us born a couple of millennia later, this verse can present some theological tension. Our minds love to take the easy way. We often avoid the tensions because it requires more work than we often want to give, but there is beauty in the deep tensions. We know God is just and merciful. We are justified by grace alone, but faith without works is dead. These principles seem contradictory to the human mind, but not when we examine the whole of the Bible, and the depth of God's character.

There is much debate about these verses among scholars, but the context provides some clues; the audience, the timing, and a growing problem with false brothers suggest this may be pointing to those who once claimed Christ yet have shown themselves false. We also see similar themes running through Hebrews 10:29-31 regarding people who professed faith yet ultimately rejected the work of the Holy Spirit. Jude characterizes them as "doubly dead" (Jude 1:12).

Keep in mind John is writing to professing believers who understand that apart from salvation in Christ, ALL sin leads to death. This is a letter directed at those in the church. The terminology is family oriented, and he previously warned of those who have distorted the gospel. We also know that he has laid out tests for true believers earlier in this book. He warns of those who are of the spirit of the antichrist (1 John 4:3), and John tells the believers of those who "went out from us, but they did not really belong to us" (1 John 2:19).

This section is about confidence in prayer and reassurance that Jesus has overcome. Satan would love to have people walk around fearful that they may commit this one sin. We need not fear, "accidently" committing the sin that leads to death when we are abiding in Christ. For Jesus took the cross and overcame death so that we could live.

"Jesus said to her, 'I am the resurrection and the life; he who believes in Me will live even if he dies'" (John 11:25).

10. Who is John speaking to in 1 John 5:16? What should we do? What is the result?

11. Evaluate your current prayer for others. Do you pray for those who are actively involved in sin? How do these verses challenge you?

DIGGING DEEPER

Pray according to God's Will
The following references are the prayers of Paul recorded in Scripture. Study the following passages and answer the questions.

Ephesians 1:15-23
Philippians 1:9-11
Colossians 1:9-14

What kind of requests does Paul make for the people he is writing to?

How do these requests line up with God's will?

Why are the kinds of requests made in these passages appropriate in praying for any circumstance?

Day Three

YOU CAN KNOW FOR SURE:
THAT YOU HAVE VICTORY OVER SIN

Read 1 John 5:18-19

A shift in authority happens when one is born of God. Before stepping into the beauty of belief in Jesus Christ, people are enslaved by the desires and fears of their flesh. But when a person goes from death to life by turning their eyes to heaven and accepting Jesus as Lord, they set aside sin and are free to live by the Spirit. The Spirit enables the believer to make a new choice; to abide in Christ and obey. They now can bow down to the only God who can lift their head and enable them to live victoriously. Love, joy, self control, and other fruits of the Spirit (Galatians 5:22-23) begin growing in a believer's life as they love and obey the One who sits over them in gracious fatherly authority.

Read Romans 6:17-18

12. Describe the change that takes place when someone is born of God.

13. How does this change your thinking about walking in victory over sin?

Read 1 John 5:18-19

14. What does John say "we know" from these two verses?

1.

2.

What role does God have?

In the Gospel of John, Jesus uses this same word to instruct others about keeping His commands. The word "protect" or "keep" here means to guard; to keep one in the state which he is.

15. Are these verses indicating a believer will reach a point of not sinning while here on earth? Why or why not? Recall a verse or two from 1 John that supports your answer.

16. When are you tempted to believe obedience is impossible?

17. Even though Satan's schemes are tempting and we live in a world energized by him, what do these verses share that gives the believer security and safety?

18. Jude 24 reminds us that Christ, "is able to keep you from stumbling and to present you blameless before the presence of His glory with great joy." As you think and contemplate this truth, what can you remember in your current circumstances?

Day Four

YOU CAN KNOW FOR SURE:
THAT JESUS IS THE WAY, THE TRUTH AND THE LIFE

Read 1 John 5:20

19. The word "true" is used 3 times in this verse. Why is the author so concerned that the readers know the truth about Christ?

20. What is the difference between knowing about God and knowing God?

According to John 17:3, eternal life is defined as knowing God and Jesus Christ. This points to knowledge of God and Christ and to a relationship with them.

21. How does 1 John 5:20 state this same truth?

"AND THIS IS ETERNAL LIFE, THAT THEY MAY KNOW YOU, THE ONLY TRUE GOD, AND JESUS CHRIST WHOM YOU HAVE SENT."

JOHN 17:3

Often times, we think of eternal life as something a believer will enjoy after they pass away and are present in heaven with Christ, but Scripture indicates that eternal life begins at the moment of salvation. The quality and experience of a believer's life here is informed and shaped by the truth they are united with God forever.

22. How has salvation reshaped your perspective and experience in life?

23. In what ways are you different today because of experiencing eternal life in Jesus Christ?

Day Five

YOU CAN KNOW FOR SURE: ETERNAL LIFE IS REAL LIFE

Read 1 John 5:20-21

Here we have the signing off of 1 John. The letter doesn't close like a typical epistle, but instead closes with a "famous last words" kind of finale. With a fatherly tone, John warns us all, "guard yourselves from idols." An idol is anything that we love or value more than God, and those temptations are always available. It can be anything that we choose to elevate above God. Idols often are good desires that we allow to take the wrong place in our lives. Idols often present as the "must haves" of life, sometimes in addition to God. I "must have" a good marriage, well-behaved children, kind friends, a clean house, in order to be settled and fulfilled. The problem is that real true life, eternal life, is never found in the lie of an idol.

24. When have you been tempted to doubt the truth about God? About Jesus Christ as the way to salvation?

25. Based on this definition, what "must haves" are you placing before God?

26. How do you combat the lies of idols and bring your thinking back to truth?

Review 1 John 5:13

The purpose of John's writing is wrapped up in this verse. His desire was for believers to be confident in the understanding of truth and their salvation and that they may have joy. Remember that John wrote this letter under the inspiration of the Holy Spirit. It is God's desire that we are confident and assured of salvation.

27. Take a moment and review your study of 1 John. Which truths have been most impactful to you? Why?

IDOLS KEEP US FROM LOVING GOD AND OTHERS IN THE RIGHT WAY. THEY TAKE OUR ATTENTION OFF OF WHAT IS REAL AND TRUE.

28. How has this study caused you to think differently about eternal life?

29. What steps can you take to keep the truth of Jesus Christ and the assurance of your salvation in the forefront of your mind?

LESSON 8
It all Matters

Welcome to the shortest books in the Bible (well, shortest by number of verses for 2 John and number of words for 3 John). As we move into 2nd and 3rd John, it will be helpful for you to think of these as memos, notes, or little messages of instruction for the weary and confused. They are not intended to be full discourses spanning all concerns of the church but are sent with the purpose of potent encouragement, and they address specific problems impacting the church.

Day One

OBEDIENCE MATTERS

1. Whose home do you enjoy spending time in? What makes it so appealing?

Read 2 John; focus on verses 1-6

Unlike 1 John this letter is composed in typical correspondence form.

2. How does John identify himself? What does this designation reveal about his role in this church and his stage of life?

It is likely that 2 John was written in Ephesus on parchment with ink in the early 90's AD. Scholars will disagree that this book is either written to a lady and her children that John knew well or this lady is a personification of a particular church and the congregants. John is quick to remind of the love he has for them and how that is coupled with truth. As we mentioned at the

---

MEMORY VERSE:

"AND THIS IS LOVE, THAT WE WALK ACCORDING TO HIS COMMANDMENTS. THIS IS THE COMMANDMENT, JUST AS YOU HAVE HEARD FROM THE BEGINNING, SO THAT YOU SHOULD WALK IN IT.

2 JOHN 6

beginning of 1 John, John never clearly identifies himself as the writer. In 1 John there was no introduction, and in 2 and 3 John he calls himself the elder. It is his language that gives him away and connects the writer of these 3 books to the writer of the Gospel of John, and that is seen even in these first three verses. Truth. Love. Abide.

3. What do you notice about his greeting?

4. What does John say love is? Why is this reminder necessary?

5. What is our obedience to God? Read John 14:15-16, 21, and 23 to help you answer this question.

6. Where in your life is God requesting obedience? How would obedience in this area help you to love others?

Day Two
TRUTH MATTERS

Read 2 John; focus on verses 7-13

It is clear that the early church, as beautiful and vibrant as it was, kept running into trials. Here in 2 John we see that false teachers were trying to lead believers astray. Gnosticism continued to gain its own supporters as the church and the gospel marched forward throughout the world. The Gnostic followers saw opportunity to share their own message that a special/secret knowledge could save, and humanity needed to be delivered from the material world. This group of antichrists (those against Christ) believed they were held back by their earthly bodies and longed for ascension from them. It is here that Gnosticism denied the Gospel most ardently, for they acknowledged the supernaturality of Jesus but would not admit that He was fully human and fully God. This began to seep into the church, and John wasn't going to stand for it!

7. What do the following verses show about Jesus' humanity?

   Matthew 4:1-2

   Matthew 26:36-38

   John 4:6-7

8. Why is it important to acknowledge Jesus' humanity?

9. What do the following verses reveal about Jesus' divinity?

John 1:1-3

John 14:6-9

Mark 2:5-7

10. Why is it important to acknowledge Jesus' divinity? Refer to John 1:22-23 for help.

11. After studying these truths, what do you think was the meaning of John's warning in verses 8-9? Remember, the Gnostics were presenting a special message that would seem more advanced or modern than Jesus' gospel. In today's culture, where might you get off track?

12. What was John's concern in verse 10? Does this mean we shouldn't let anyone who disagrees with us into our house?

13. How can we love well and still heed John's warning?

Day Three
HOSPITALITY MATTERS

Third John is a short personal note to a friend and partner in ministry to remind of the role hospitality and love have in empowering the momentum of evangelism. John also warns that not all people of the early church are worth imitating. Some are self–seeking and are hindering the gospel with their response to those who are voyaging out to share it. He offers his friend simple but profound advice—imitate what is good.

Read 3 John 1-15
---

14. There are three key people John mentions in his note. Record all that you can about these four individuals. Consider their actions, attitudes, emotions and circumstances.

Gaius—

Diotrephes—

Demetrius—

Read 3 John 1-15

15. John commended Gaius for waking in truth, being faithful, loving the church and caring for strangers. John was especially thankful for the hospitality Gaius had shown. Who did Gaius show hospitality to, and what did he do to demonstrate his hospitality (verse 5-8)?

THE PHRASE "SEND THEM ON THEIR JOURNEY" REFERS TO SENDING WITH NECESSARY MATERIAL AND SUPPORT FOR THE JOURNEY.

16. In what ways is the hospitality John refers to in 2 John 10-11 different than the hospitality he refers to in 3 John 5-8?

DIGGING DEEPER

Consider the following passages and how biblical hospitality is shown. What characteristics do we discover about biblical hospitality? How does biblical hospitality differ from entertaining?

Judges 19:1-4

2 Samuel 17:27-29

Matthew 26:6-13

Luke 19:1-10

Day Four

HUMILITY MATTERS

Read 3 John 9-10

John's letter turns quickly from commending Gaius to condemning Diotrephes. John is clearly upset because Diotrphes is standing in the way of the spread of the Gospel because of his lack of humility.

17. What is motivating Diotrephes? What is he doing that demonstrates his motivation?

Diotrephes was not alone in his desire to be first. James , and even John, at one time had the same problem when they requested to be seated at the right and left hand of Jesus.

Read Mark 10:35-45

18. How did Jesus respond to their request? What really matters to Jesus?

"...BUT WHOEVER WOULD BE GREAT AMONG YOU MUST BE YOUR SERVANT, AND WHOEVER WOULD BE FIRST AMONG YOU MUST BE SLAVE OF ALL."
MARK 10:43B-44

19. Evaluate your own motivation. Do you desire to be first, to be recognized, to be the center of attention in any area? Consider your relationships, your career and your ministry. Confess if necessary.

20. Review the example of Gaius in verses 5-8. John told him to send those that had spent time with him on their journey in a manner "worthy of God," encouraging him to treat them in the same way Jesus would. Consider Jesus' example in Philippians 2:3-8. How would your attitude and actions change if you treated others as "worthy of God?"

Day Five

INTEGRITY MATTERS

Read 3 John 11-15

As John is wrapping up his note, he does not miss the opportunity to address the believers of Gaius's church.

21. What instructions does he give (verse 11)?

22. John expanded on this thought earlier in 1 John 3:6-10. what does "imitating good" look and act like?

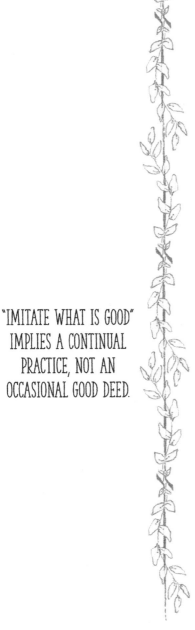

"IMITATE WHAT IS GOOD" IMPLIES A CONTINUAL PRACTICE, NOT AN OCCASIONAL GOOD DEED.

23. "Imitating good" results in others noticing. Who had noticed Demetrius and what was their report?

24. Who do you know that faithfully "imitates good"? Consider writing them a note of appreciation for their faithful testimony.

25. What does John's salutation (verse 13-15) reveal about his genuine love and care? Who has God placed in your life to love and care for in this way?

Through the writings of John, we have been challenged to walk in the light and reflect the brilliant colors of God's character. This challenge has included opportunities to test ourselves, to put a mirror up to our hearts and discover the genuineness of our love, the depth of our desire to live in obedience and the strength of our dedication to following the true Jesus.

26. What recurring themes have you seen?

27. In what areas have you been personally challenged?

NOTES

1. The Gospel Transformation Bible, Crossway, Wheaton, IL

2. 1,2, 3 John and Jude, MacAurthur, Thomas Nelson, 2007, page 16

Appendix: 1-3 John

1 John

1 That which was from the beginning, which we have heard, which we have seen with our eyes, which we looked upon and have touched with our hands, concerning the word of life— ² the life was made manifest, and we have seen it, and testify to it and proclaim to you the eternal life, which was with the Father and was made manifest to us— ³ that which we have seen and heard we proclaim also to you, so that you too may have fellowship with us; and indeed our fellowship is with the Father and with his Son Jesus Christ. ⁴ And we are writing these things so that our joy may be complete.

⁵ This is the message we have heard from him and proclaim to you, that God is light, and in him is no darkness at all. ⁶ If we say we have fellowship with him while we walk in darkness, we lie and do not practice the truth. ⁷ But if we walk in the light, as he is in the light, we have fellowship with one another, and the blood of Jesus his Son cleanses us from all sin. ⁸ If we say we have no sin, we deceive ourselves, and the truth is not in us. ⁹ If we confess our sins, he is faithful and just to forgive us our sins and to cleanse us from all unrighteousness. ¹⁰ If we say we have not sinned, we make him a liar, and his word is not in us.

2 My little children, I am writing these things to you so that you may not sin. But if anyone does sin, we have an advocate with the Father, Jesus Christ the righteous. ² He is the propitiation for our sins, and not for ours only but also for the sins of the whole world. ³ And by this we know that we have come to know him, if we keep his commandments. ⁴ Whoever says "I know him" but does not keep his commandments is a liar, and the truth is not in him, ⁵ but whoever keeps his word, in him truly the love of God is perfected. By this we may know that we are in him: ⁶ whoever says he abides in him ought to walk in the same way in which he walked.

⁷ Beloved, I am writing you no new commandment, but an old commandment that you had from the beginning. The old commandment is the word that you have heard. ⁸ At the same time, it is a new commandment that I am writing to you, which is true in him and in you, because the darkness is passing away and the true light is already shining. ⁹ Whoever says he is in the light and hates his brother is still in darkness. ¹⁰ Whoever loves his brother abides in the light, and in him there is no cause for stumbling. ¹¹ But whoever hates his brother is in the darkness and walks in the darkness, and does not know where he is going, because the darkness has blinded his eyes.

¹² I am writing to you, little children,
    because your sins are forgiven for his name's sake.
¹³ I am writing to you, fathers,
    because you know him who is from the beginning.
I am writing to you, young men,
    because you have overcome the evil one.
I write to you, children,
    because you know the Father.
¹⁴ I write to you, fathers,

because you know him who is from the beginning.
I write to you, young men,
    because you are strong,
    and the word of God abides in you,
    and you have overcome the evil one.

15 Do not love the world or the things in the world. If anyone loves the world, the love of the Father is not in him. 16 For all that is in the world—the desires of the flesh and the desires of the eyes and pride of life—is not from the Father but is from the world. 17 And the world is passing away along with its desires, but whoever does the will of God abides forever.

18 Children, it is the last hour, and as you have heard that antichrist is coming, so now many antichrists have come. Therefore we know that it is the last hour. 19 They went out from us, but they were not of us; for if they had been of us, they would have continued with us. But they went out, that it might become plain that they all are not of us. 20 But you have been anointed by the Holy One, and you all have knowledge. 21 I write to you, not because you do not know the truth, but because you know it, and because no lie is of the truth. 22 Who is the liar but he who denies that Jesus is the Christ? This is the antichrist, he who denies the Father and the Son. 23 No one who denies the Son has the Father. Whoever confesses the Son has the Father also. 24 Let what you heard from the beginning abide in you. If what you heard from the beginning abides in you, then you too will abide in the Son and in the Father. 25 And this is the promise that he made to us—eternal life.

26 I write these things to you about those who are trying to deceive you. 27 But the anointing that you received from him abides in you, and you have no need that anyone should teach you. But as his anointing teaches you about everything, and is true, and is no lie—just as it has taught you, abide in him.

28 And now, little children, abide in him, so that when he appears we may have confidence and not shrink from him in shame at his coming. 29 If you know that he is righteous, you may be sure that everyone who practices righteousness has been born of him.

3 See what kind of love the Father has given to us, that we should be called children of God; and so we are. The reason why the world does not know us is that it did not know him. 2 Beloved, we are God's children now, and what we will be has not yet appeared; but we know that when he appears we shall be like him, because we shall see him as he is. 3 And everyone who thus hopes in him purifies himself as he is pure.

4 Everyone who makes a practice of sinning also practices lawlessness; sin is lawlessness. 5 You know that he appeared in order to take away sins, and in him there is no sin. 6 No one who abides in him keeps on sinning; no one who keeps on sinning has either seen him or known him. 7 Little children, let no one deceive you. Whoever practices righteousness is righteous, as he is righteous. 8 Whoever makes a practice of sinning is of the devil, for the devil has been sinning from the beginning. The reason the Son of God appeared was to destroy the works of the devil. 9 No one born of God makes a practice of sinning, for God's seed abides in him; and he cannot keep on sinning, because he has been born of God. 10 By this it is evident who are the children of God, and who are the children of the devil: whoever does not practice righteousness is not of God, nor is the one who does not love his brother.

11 For this is the message that you have heard from the beginning, that we should love one another. 12 We should not be like Cain, who was of the evil one and murdered his brother.

And why did he murder him? Because his own deeds were evil and his brother's righteous. ¹³ Do not be surprised, brothers, that the world hates you. ¹⁴ We know that we have passed out of death into life, because we love the brothers. Whoever does not love abides in death. ¹⁵ Everyone who hates his brother is a murderer, and you know that no murderer has eternal life abiding in him.

¹⁶ By this we know love, that he laid down his life for us, and we ought to lay down our lives for the brothers. ¹⁷ But if anyone has the world's goods and sees his brother in need, yet closes his heart against him, how does God's love abide in him? ¹⁸ Little children, let us not love in word or talk but in deed and in truth.

¹⁹ By this we shall know that we are of the truth and reassure our heart before him; ²⁰ for whenever our heart condemns us, God is greater than our heart, and he knows everything. ²¹ Beloved, if our heart does not condemn us, we have confidence before God; ²² and whatever we ask we receive from him, because we keep his commandments and do what pleases him. ²³ And this is his commandment, that we believe in the name of his Son Jesus Christ and love one another, just as he has commanded us. ²⁴ Whoever keeps his commandments abides in God, and God in him. And by this we know that he abides in us, by the Spirit whom he has given us.

⁴ Beloved, do not believe every spirit, but test the spirits to see whether they are from God, for many false prophets have gone out into the world. ² By this you know the Spirit of God: every spirit that confesses that Jesus Christ has come in the flesh is from God, ³ and every spirit that does not confess Jesus is not from God. This is the spirit of the antichrist, which you heard was coming and now is in the world already. ⁴ Little children, you are from God and have overcome them, for he who is in you is greater than he who is in the world. ⁵ They are from the world; therefore they speak from the world, and the world listens to them. ⁶ We are from God. Whoever knows God listens to us; whoever is not from God does not listen to us. By this we know the Spirit of truth and the spirit of error.

⁷ Beloved, let us love one another, for love is from God, and whoever loves has been born of God and knows God. ⁸ Anyone who does not love does not know God, because God is love. ⁹ In this the love of God was made manifest among us, that God sent his only Son into the world, so that we might live through him. ¹⁰ In this is love, not that we have loved God but that he loved us and sent his Son to be the propitiation for our sins. ¹¹ Beloved, if God so loved us, we also ought to love one another. ¹² No one has ever seen God; if we love one another, God abides in us and his love is perfected in us.

¹³ By this we know that we abide in him and he in us, because he has given us of his Spirit. ¹⁴ And we have seen and testify that the Father has sent his Son to be the Savior of the world. ¹⁵ Whoever confesses that Jesus is the Son of God, God abides in him, and he in God. ¹⁶ So we have come to know and to believe the love that God has for us. God is love, and whoever abides in love abides in God, and God abides in him. ¹⁷ By this is love perfected with us, so that we may have confidence for the day of judgment, because as he is so also are we in this world. ¹⁸ There is no fear in love, but perfect love casts out fear. For fear has to do with punishment, and whoever fears has not been perfected in love. ¹⁹ We love because he first loved us. ²⁰ If anyone says, "I love God," and hates his brother, he is a liar; for he who does not love his brother whom he has seen cannot love God whom he has not seen. ²¹ And this commandment we have from him: whoever loves God must also love his brother.

⁵ Everyone who believes that Jesus is the Christ has been born of God, and everyone who

loves the Father loves whoever has been born of him. [2] By this we know that we love the children of God, when we love God and obey his commandments. [3] For this is the love of God, that we keep his commandments. And his commandments are not burdensome. [4] For everyone who has been born of God overcomes the world. And this is the victory that has overcome the world—our faith. [5] Who is it that overcomes the world except the one who believes that Jesus is the Son of God?

[6] This is he who came by water and blood—Jesus Christ; not by the water only but by the water and the blood. And the Spirit is the one who testifies, because the Spirit is the truth. [7] For there are three that testify: [8] the Spirit and the water and the blood; and these three agree. [9] If we receive the testimony of men, the testimony of God is greater, for this is the testimony of God that he has borne concerning his Son. [10] Whoever believes in the Son of God has the testimony in himself. Whoever does not believe God has made him a liar, because he has not believed in the testimony that God has borne concerning his Son. [11] And this is the testimony, that God gave us eternal life, and this life is in his Son. [12] Whoever has the Son has life; whoever does not have the Son of God does not have life.

[13] I write these things to you who believe in the name of the Son of God, that you may know that you have eternal life. [14] And this is the confidence that we have toward him, that if we ask anything according to his will he hears us. [15] And if we know that he hears us in whatever we ask, we know that we have the requests that we have asked of him.

[16] If anyone sees his brother committing a sin not leading to death, he shall ask, and God will give him life—to those who commit sins that do not lead to death. There is sin that leads to death; I do not say that one should pray for that. [17] All wrongdoing is sin, but there is sin that does not lead to death.

[18] We know that everyone who has been born of God does not keep on sinning, but he who was born of God protects him, and the evil one does not touch him.

[19] We know that we are from God, and the whole world lies in the power of the evil one.

[20] And we know that the Son of God has come and has given us understanding, so that we may know him who is true; and we are in him who is true, in his Son Jesus Christ. He is the true God and eternal life. [21] Little children, keep yourselves from idols.

2 John

[1] The elder to the elect lady and her children, whom I love in truth, and not only I, but also all who know the truth, [2] because of the truth that abides in us and will be with us forever:

[3] Grace, mercy, and peace will be with us, from God the Father and from Jesus Christ the Father's Son, in truth and love.

[4] I rejoiced greatly to find some of your children walking in the truth, just as we were commanded by the Father. [5] And now I ask you, dear lady—not as though I were writing you a new commandment, but the one we have had from the beginning—that we love one another. [6] And this is love, that we walk according to his commandments; this is the commandment, just as you have heard from the beginning, so that you should walk in it. [7] For many deceivers have gone out into the world, those who do not confess the coming of Jesus Christ in the flesh. Such a one is the deceiver and the antichrist. [8] Watch yourselves, so that you may not lose what we have worked for, but may win a full reward. [9] Everyone who goes on ahead and does not abide in the teaching of Christ, does not have God.

Whoever abides in the teaching has both the Father and the Son. ¹⁰ If anyone comes to you and does not bring this teaching, do not receive him into your house or give him any greeting, ¹¹ for whoever greets him takes part in his wicked works. ¹² Though I have much to write to you, I would rather not use paper and ink. Instead I hope to come to you and talk face to face, so that our joy may be complete.

¹³ The children of your elect sister greet you.

3 John

¹ The elder to the beloved Gaius, whom I love in truth.

² Beloved, I pray that all may go well with you and that you may be in good health, as it goes well with your soul. ³ For I rejoiced greatly when the brothers came and testified to your truth, as indeed you are walking in the truth. ⁴ I have no greater joy than to hear that my children are walking in the truth.

⁵ Beloved, it is a faithful thing you do in all your efforts for these brothers, strangers as they are, ⁶ who testified to your love before the church. You will do well to send them on their journey in a manner worthy of God. ⁷ For they have gone out for the sake of the name, accepting nothing from the Gentiles. ⁸ Therefore we ought to support people like these, that we may be fellow workers for the truth.

⁹ I have written something to the church, but Diotrephes, who likes to put himself first, does not acknowledge our authority. ¹⁰ So if I come, I will bring up what he is doing, talking wicked nonsense against us. And not content with that, he refuses to welcome the brothers, and also stops those who want to and puts them out of the church.

¹¹ Beloved, do not imitate evil but imitate good. Whoever does good is from God; whoever does evil has not seen God. ¹² Demetrius has received a good testimony from everyone, and from the truth itself. We also add our testimony, and you know that our testimony is true.

¹³ I had much to write to you, but I would rather not write with pen and ink. ¹⁴ I hope to see you soon, and we will talk face to face.

¹⁵ Peace be to you. The friends greet you. Greet the friends, each by name.

Made in the USA
Monee, IL
05 September 2021